A THOUSAND
THREADS

ALSO BY STEVE ORLEN

A THOUSAND THREADS

A Chapbook

Steve Orlen

Hollyridge Press
Venice, California

Hollyridge Press
P.O. Box 2872
Venice, California 90294
www.hollyridgepress.com

Cover and Book Design by Rio Smyth
Cover Image "Sarah" ©Eric Kroll
Author photo by Gail Marcus-Orlen
Manufactured in the United States of America by Lightning Source

ISBN-13: 978-0-9843100-2-9
ISBN-10: 0-9843100-2-9

Grateful acknowledgment is made to the editors of the following
publications where these poems first appeared:

Alhambra Poetry Calendar 2009: "Ninth Avenue"
The Gettysburg Review: "Slovenia"
It's Not You, It's Me, edited by Jerry Williams (The Overlook Press)*:* "A Man
   Alone"
The Massachusetts Review: "The Years Between the Wars"
New England Review: "A Poet's Job"; "Hurricane"; "Something Blindly
   Unexpected"
New Ohio Review: "I Enter an Ancient City in a Dream"

16 15 14 13 12 11 10 09   10 9 8 7 6 5 4 3 2 1

Contents

A THOUSAND THREADS

IN SPRING

At one end, the tongue, at the other a stinger. In between
A flying machine that bears the bee from flower to flower,
From field to hive, the fat Queen. The boy picking flowers
In the field is in love with his teacher who's in love
With the carpenter, who loves her, and her sister, too,
Who loves the field and the flowers but is scared of bees.
In the field, it's morning for the boy, evening for the teacher
Making love with her lover, night for her sister
Who wears long black gloves and a long dress, also black,
So as not to be mistaken for either flower or lover.
Over them all, the fat Queen rises with a drone (who will
Die when it's done) and they mate on the wing.

DEATH OF A LYRIC POET

The villagers spiral up the hill and gather just below the tree
Where the priest spreads the ashes, and recites the simple ritual,
And a few mothers distribute sweets. The children are delighted—
The strange man, their teacher, finally gone and the land
Can rest again for years to come—Street of Winter will be The Road,
Path of Birds The River. Afterwards, spiraling down the hill,
Some few men take from their pockets a lemon,
And some few women linger by the gates, chewing on onions.

NINTH AVENUE

The late hour, her walk, slow, high-heeled, and the way her dress
Swirled as though pleased with itself, suggested a woman I once knew.
I called out a name, she glanced at me, she disappeared into a
    doorway.
Then I was even surer she was who I thought she was. But had I ever
Actually known her, or was she someone I'd seen on a similar street
In another city often enough to give me that feeling, the way
    mere possibility
Can find its way into memory and get snared in the fabric? I
    looked around.
I could have been anywhere, a young man in a big city, in that zone
Of the temporarily lost, on a dreary street outside a Laundromat
Next to a bar locking its doors. Nothing that happens gets erased.
Someone is stopped in a déjà vu and marks the spot. There are names
Carved into trees. We stop to decipher them for a few moments,
And walk away feeling thoughtful, not sure why.

I ENTER AN ANCIENT CITY IN A DREAM

I had a dream in which I enter an ancient city by The Poet's Gate.
I see fountains of the clearest waters, and statues
Tall as ships' masts. The winds blow the sands of history
Down every street and clog my ears and sting my eyes.
I stop a priest and ask, "How old is this metropolis?"
"Our city was founded long before we counted time in years.
What lies underground we cannot know, except a thousand
Thousand dynasties have been compressed like grapes
And the wine turned dry as dust." "I'm a poet," I tell him.
"I've wandered everywhere and learned of great sages,
And immortals with powers I never imagined,
But I like to know about the common people, too. Carriers
Of water, and dung gatherers and those sand sweepers
Bent into question marks—how do they fare here?"
"They live and die, like everywhere, when the gods aren't listening.
You, poet, look to thyself. Your dream has carried you far,
And now you stand upon millennia of sand, and want to know
About the little man? Ask me a better question than that."

THE MUSEUM OF WORK

Black, high-topped, leather boots as new as when a Polish soldier
Broke them in, September, 1939, running toward a German tank,
Then wised up and ran back home and hid them under the
    chicken coop.
His son wore them across the ocean. They walked him to school.
They pushed the pedal of a big dump truck, and in those boots
He bought three more trucks, then sat for forty years in a
    cramped office,
Like an American, doing the numbers that made the money
We call *The Great American Success Story.*
A pair of boots, humiliated in war and redeemed by work.
Now on display in The Museum of Work, next to the ladders.

HARD LABOR

When they first presented her with the baby she said, *I don't ever*
Want to see this fucking thing again. The next day she relented,
And with stiff arms received the soft and weightless bundle,
Glared away her husband and the nurse. She stroked the fontanel
And looked inside. A cloud swirled. Snow was falling. A fat baby
Spun around on a spike, slower and slower. She turned it over
And shook it a bit, and started it snowing again. The baby spun.
I remember an old woman so angry at her son she threatened
To "put him back where he came from." In Rome, the nursing mother
Of a bastard child would smear her breasts with opium. In Herod's
Massacre of the innocents, all were slain except the one he aimed for.

THE YEARS BETWEEN WARS

The border river is just as measly on one side
As on the other. You can see a teenage girl tying
White strips of cloth on the lowest branches of an oak,
Which spreads its leafy shadows half-way across,
And only the falling leaves
Remember the rest of the way. On the other side,
A girl stops on a path and knots
A string around her thumb, and that's
The only difference anyone remembers because
The boundary was drawn three wars ago
By an emperor who never set foot here.
Which people he gathered into his empire,
Which he left out, doesn't matter because
There are no people on maps,
And because there is no empire anymore, and those
Who moved away are already American dust.
My great-grandfather traveled
For the first time across an ocean to lay flowers
And prayers on some graves, and when he stepped into the river
To cross to the grave of his great-grandmother,
An old woman with a pitchfork waved him back.
On both sides, the emperor's name is mud,
The women, when they are pretty, are just as pretty,
And the brandy is made of plums.

THE MIDDLE ROOM

Are you implying that half of our dilemma
Is that we got used to the struggle that pits desire
Against fulfillment, and the other is the struggle
To forget we got used to it, so that, for example,
The view across a city, if it's beautiful,
Will be beautiful tomorrow, but will seem new?
"No," she says. "We don't have that problem.
I sleep on this side of the bed, you on the other.
Between us there's always another room,
And some nights I turn to watch these two people,
Strangers to each other, and they're making love
In terror and with abandon." Are you implying
That we're bored, and that we've opted out
Of the tension between desire and fulfillment,
Or that I should meet you there, and watch
And learn some new tricks? "No, I mean
We struggle to remember the moment
Before we met, when we still had dreams
And didn't know they were about to be
Broken and subsumed by a stranger. Then the thousand,
And the thousand thousand threads unraveling."

THE MARRIAGE OF ECHO & NARCISSUS

He is having sex, earnestly, trying to learn how, and she
Is making love, lovingly, believing she's in love
Because incapable of duplicity.

He won't speak, except to ask, *Who are you?*
She can only echo, like a child, *Who are you?*

As long as he doesn't answer, he doesn't know,
And as long as she pines for the one who isn't there,
They'll stay like this forever,
Working through the paradigm, trying to get it right.

AN OLD MAN'S SENSUAL NIGHTS

When the night outside his window is blank of stars and it's raining
Cats and dogs like it used to rain, he masturbates, from memory.
The women arrive in parts—so much time has passed—they drift.
Breast of the goddess in stone he once put his mouth around.
He savors the ancient taste. Vagina in a hand-mirror, examining itself.
Naked with a woman all morning on a beach beside a lake, her areoles
Of inconstant light. Nothing whole enough to speak the words
    of love to,
Or regret, or ask for more, and more. An old man's prick, pressed
Between his legs, restless, visionary, an audience, happy and unapologetic,
Even in defeat. A passing labia licks his tongue. A mouth retreats,
    descends.

THE STENDHAL SYNDROME:
VENCE, FRANCE

Is beauty in the mind or in the object? is not a sensible question.
Kant hadn't met the Hungarian Countess Karolyi, ninety-one,
Who lingered, leaning on a slender cane, in front of her chateau
With the humbled grace of Royalty in exile over half a century.
Her smile had flown all the way from a palace in Budapest
To greet me. I thought I might pass out and fall down
In the wildflowers, from overexposure
To her enduring and transient beauty. It was raining,
A boy stood beside her holding a red umbrella
Shaped like a bell jar. Stendhal,
When he saw Giotto's sublime frescoes at Santa Croce,
Had palpitations of the heart and almost fainted.
I started to walk towards her, wondering
If we were meant to fall in love in 1923
Before her fall from grace, when an enemy wrote,
Her voluptuous young mouth smiled in rapture,
Or today.

THE TREES

The trees, the trees, the only beauties that can compare with a woman's.
In grade school, Miss McFaul taught us that the roots mirror the tree,
And underground is where decisions get made. Where
The eyeless worms' paths followed by the trickling water
Redirect the roots. A pebble dropped in place
A hundred-twenty thousand years ago by a glacier
Awakened from its long sleep. It's spring. New branches
Crisscross older branches at teenage angles.
They tangle up, you can't see anything. But a woman's beauty
    is constant,
If constantly beheld. Sixty years, and the mirror she looks into
Every morning changes nothing.

GUSTAVE VIGLAND PARK: OSLO

"What's the name of this place?" she asks. She wonders
If the journey was longer from one place to another
Before the places were given names. I love this woman.
When she talks like that I listen to the undersongs of birds
And remember the million childhood shocks of revelation
That needed no proof. (I idled near a doorway watching the guests
Leave a party. I didn't know her. She was with her lover.
I shook her hand, and she thought, *I know you're going to
Come looking for me.*) "When you leave
A place you love," she asks, "does your spirit leave behind
A few photons to guide you when you come back?" She points
To the light a sparrow's shadow left on the grass as it flew away.

ROMA TERMINI

The woman she looks like was a woman he'd been crazily in love with
Forty years ago, who hadn't loved him, but once was tempted enough
Or kind enough or cruel enough to kiss him in front of her door
With a passion that has lasted all these years, and at the end, *Someday*
Maybe, is what she said. Her umbrella, folded. Her lipstick, bright red,
Gleaming. Not a year has been added to her years. Too late. Too late.

Now you, who believe you have outgrown the juvenilia of your dreams,
Observe this man. He stands by himself on a station platform
Still waiting for his kiss, overwhelmed by the small damages
Our histories do to us, how memory retards us with its generous gifts,
Then, when it most matters, takes them back.

THE FRAGRANCE WHEEL

She takes it into her mouth, your middle finger, and licks it,
Nips it, sucks it, then slides it out and moves it down
And guides it inside to ferret out the spot, *There, oh yes,*
And after an unspoken, pleasing while, she slides the puppet out,
You talk a little, drink the last of the wine, she gets dressed,
She gently shuts the door. What lingers, after? What sadness?
What funkiness rises in the air and slowly takes the room by force?

You slide it under your nose, your finger, back and forth,
Apprentice perfumier, oenologist, sous chef. Essence
Of the untweaked blossoms of the ginkgo and the tree of heaven.
Haze of smoke in a jazz cafe with more or less top notes and bass.
And sour milk, urine, bath of vinegar and common sweat,
And guiding the mix, the cruel, blind endlessness
Of outer space made inner, without you, without the man.

ANYTHING BIG

The grace of the very tall woman gliding past the iron workers
On their lunch break, silences their whistles. And when I asked
    the physicist
About the concept of infinity, he excited himself out of the
    mathematical
Into the spiritual. Anything big, huge, outsized, fascinates,
    though not that farmer
Who made a ball of string tall as the barn eaves, not the Romans
Who traveled island to island seeking the race of giants they
    knew did not exist
So they could defeat them and found an empire on a myth.
I mean that football player in line at the movie theater. I stood
    as close
As I could get to his immensity to feel what in me it might excite,
And what came took my breath away: Some days before he
    died, Shelley
Met his doppelganger in a dream,
Who asked, *How long do you mean to be content?*

SLOVENIA

I napped, woke, napped again, and when the bus pulled over,
    woke again.
Not a light to be seen, only the dark and mostly starless sky above us
And on both sides of the road, dark wooded walls that earlier
    were forest.

You see them everywhere in the Balkans, these women, placid, ageless,
Dressed from head to toe in black. She stood and stepped off the bus.
The driver waited. Individual trees emerged, they looked like shadows,
And not in rows, not a path to be seen anywhere between them.

Every so often I see her when I'm falling asleep, a robe of black
Entering a forest equally black. Surely someone, somewhere
In those airless woods was waiting for her.

HURRICANE

When his father says, *Think before you speak*, it's like telling a clown
To be serious for once. Like telling an actor to freeze long
    moments on a stage
And reconsider the lines he's memorized. Like telling the color yellow
To tone it down for the funeral. The boy is eleven. It's hard to think
With the noisy rain still coming down in buckets. Last night a hurricane
Slammed the street and in the morning the boy's uncle stopped by
In a canoe, waving a paddle, and big trees were upended, every-
    one could see
What made a tree a tree.
                          Across the street, in front of the pharmacy
With his friends, someone's blond, and beautiful, visiting older sister
Leaned down and kissed him on the lips.
All stories, explosive as a storm or ordinary as a walk, lose in
    the telling.
Lose everything, in fact. The lips go slack. The clean smell of
    the small
Puff of breath dissolves. His uncle is a man who works in a garage.
What's left is a great noise in the night that took all other
    noise away.

ENTRYWAY IN SHADOW

In Rome, on the Piazza di Spagna, a young Italian man. They
    made love
In his attic room off the Via Anselmo. "Funny to remember
    that," she says,
"But not his name. I was seventeen." She named the baby *Anselmo*.
Half his mother and half the entire land of Italy.
Forty years pass. The lover takes his Sunday morning walk
When it comes back to him: her rounded, wholesome
Pale American body furious above his own. For a week,
Clairvoyant resonances turn up everywhere he looks:
His shadow, eclipsing a bright entryway.
Footprints in the snow, the mailman come and gone.
That's not unusual. In all of us the same thing has gone missing.

WHAT MUSIC MEASURES

A meadow, recently mown, and vast. I couldn't see
The end of it, and I can't say the exact moment because
I was daydreaming when the fiddle started up,
Mid-tune of an Appalachian tune. I couldn't see
Where it was coming from, neither instrument nor player.
I could hear it, but as soon as it was swallowed by my ears
It was gone to wherever in the mind music goes
As one passage replaces another. Note after note, lively
As they first burst up from the fiddle, and as they rose
They diminished, and, as beauty has its limits, disappeared
Without an echo to remember them by. When the music stopped,
Meadow, sky, all of it seemed dull without whatever it was
The music had measured.

A MAN ALONE

He hated breaking up and he hated being left, finding himself
    in an apartment
With an extra set of silverware and a ghost, impatient to be gone.
Then to summon up who he was before the bed was full with woman.
To shift the street-mind from *getting to* to *slowing down and*
    window shop.
In the bar, to let his eyes simplify again, and make no judgments,
And breathe in the smoke that drifts through one body then another,
And find himself close enough to whisper into a woman's just-
    washed hair
And inhale that ten thousand year old scent. To keep his hands
    in his pockets,
Like a boy. To open the heart, only a little at a time. To say
    goodnight at her door.

ANOREXIC

On the shoreline, the woman lounged, topless, oiling
Her already dark, insistent, global tan.
Squeezed into the razor thinness of her profile,
She looked like someone missing among the fleshly.
Her breasts, reduced to ornaments, and each rib
Waited to be counted. When I passed by, she adjusted
Her posture, she smiled up at me, as though proud
Of what she had to offer, and at that moment
Her hip bones broke forth from her body
Like the prow of a ship that had suddenly
Emerged from the sand, its hull stripped
To a skeleton, and all its sailors drowned.

ARIA

I can't remember the name, the German movie in which a terribly
    homely woman
Is preparing her breakfast, eats it, reads the paper, cleans the
    kitchen in one long scene
Of maybe thirty minutes. One of those women you pass in the grocery
And wish the world were a fairer place. But she was stark naked
And I couldn't take my eyes off her body. The body, let's just
    say it was beautiful.
And a face that made you want to turn away. And if we could
    see it, what about the soul?
Nine parts the purity of heaven's breath, one part smudged
    with life.
Like those dark areas in an x-ray. The technician leans in
And squints, unsure whether they're signatures of your death, or
    irregularities,
Or he hasn't learned how to read them yet.
To remain alive in this world takes a careful attentiveness.
In the upstairs apartment, that aria
Unwinding from an old recording so scratched you can't tell
Whether you're listening to song or scream.

DOPPELGANGER

"You know what I mean. You're just like me," she says,
From her pillow to his, a remark that always jams into his brain
Its sliver of doubt, then slides its arm around his shoulders.

Then comes that familiar, enticing inner other who whispers,
When you most need it, *You're not alone after all.*

He goes back to his apartment and for hours is visited by images.
Colonies of bees, the long-married, the faces of their dogs.

TUSCANY

It's those narrow passageways, the stone lanes that smell as dark
As their histories of adultery and murder, that make time slow down
Like a tower clock in an abandoned village in the mountains.
Head down, walking toward me, a girl is hugging her heavy
    school books.
Her long, straight black hair needs trimming. My coat brushes
Against the wall on my side and I don't say anything.
I don't want to scare her with my maleness. When I was
    young, silence would
Intimidate a woman. They thought I was brooding. Some
    women loved that.
To be menaced and seduced by an unbearable silence they took
    to be profound,
Maybe even spiritual. *Which way to the fire?* is what I was thinking.
What's unbearable now is a young Italian schoolgirl, her hair like
Strands of silk drying outside a factory, walking past without even
Glancing up to see if I'm someone to be scared of.

A WAITRESS ON HER SMOKE BREAK

With all his Frenchnness, he leans toward her. "Je toi desire," he says,
And she takes a deep drag off her cigarette. Americans are a
    blunter people.
Better off not to say anything when the object of desire
Is close enough to kiss. When the first French sailor got off the
    ship at Pevensey
And said to the first bar-maid, *Je toi desire*, she knew what she
    was in for
Because the words had floated in on the tides a hundred years before.

When Americans think *desire*, we mean *ache for, yearn for*.
The endless, hushed roaring of its river in the distance
Will make a little girl try on her mother's bra on a rainy day,
    and an old man
Strip to the bone and float from New Jersey down to Florida,
And a poet renew the contract with the spiritual. The young Frenchman
Is testing the American waters. The waitress will make him wait.
She will profit from his ignorance and from her own.

A POET'S JOB

No one deadheaded her roses this fall. Her chickens are missing
From the backyard trees. I don't get to hear her irritating
    smoker's cough
Crack crack through the oleander hedge between our houses late
    at night.
I woke up last night with Donne's words on my mind:
Every death diminishes me. "Adelia here," she said one night,
Calling me to the curb. Midnight. Moonlight. Stars.
Two coyotes, a male and female, trotted like self-aggrandized
    dogs toward us
Down the middle of the street toward the park at the end
Where the prey are plentiful and small.
Urbanized, not looking at us. I hate that big-city haughty indifference.
At night, when a tiny death squeal racks the silence like a toy siren,
The neighborhood diminishes and I am left looking at the moon
Which, as someone must have said, exposes everything
But sheds no light of its own. To go out and look at the moon
Has been a poet's job at least since the first Sumerian poet
Compared the color of grazing cows
To the risen moon, and their multitude to the stars.
To look at the stars and ponder the countless human verities.
Sometimes one is enough. After one Adelia, there are no more.

MATTERS OF FAITH

I do not regret anything at all, either the good
that has been done to me or the evil
Everything is equal to me

When Edith Piaf sang *Je ne regrette rien*,
Was she lying, for the sake of song?
What can we say about this woman, in whom
Recollected pain, and kindness, too,
Were no longer in proportion to their intensity?
Was it the wisdom of experience? The numbness
Of the aged romantic? Had she stood too long in the rain?
In Paris, it's always raining when she sings.
It's a law of nature. That street-worn, orphaned voice
Eulogized love, even as it bloomed; and of the weather,
She sang *Beautiful day, it's raining.*
She was refused a Catholic burial mass by the Archbishop
Of Paris who abhorred her multitude of sins.
Would he have felt absolved by her almost indifferent generosity,
Even as he gave his verdict? She was so tiny.
If you passed her in Belleville singing on the street,
A sooty sparrow, and offered the crumbs of your baguette,
Would she have written a song effacing the difference
Between large and small acts of beneficence?
Je ne regrette rien. She was no saint,
Whose suffering made her indifferent
To whatever life offers. She wasn't the type

To turn the other cheek. She wasn't the concubine
Of a bodhisattva, but a delivery boy, a boxer, and a pimp.
I haven't asked a Frenchman what she meant.
You would have to be on your deathbed
To answer such a question.

NOT KIN

Who remembers the story of an ordinary fight
Over something stupid with my best friend,
In the driveway and we were both getting in some good ones,
Until his mother on the third-story porch about to hang her laundry
Started yelling *Kill him Arno, kill him*, over and over,
Until it didn't sound human anymore and she was a crowd of
     women
At an execution site urging the hangman on. That happens all
     the time.
Your wife takes your mother's side in an argument with you.
My mother saying that if it came down to it she'd save my
     father from drowning
Before she'd save my brother and me. A woman I'd known almost
     all my short life
Was siccing her son on me like a dog, a junkyard dog.
Once Arno was in an accident, his head smashed through the
     windshield,
It took hours for the surgeons to get out all the glass.
Ten years later, we were talking, he grabbed
His handkerchief and blew his nose, and out came a sliver of
     glass.
That's the story someone will tell for the rest of his life.

`

COMMONPLACE

They were making love in the middle
Of the afternoon, and the slats of sunlight
Across the bed made her feel exposed,
So they stopped. He thought how differently
Beautiful a naked woman looks
When sex is no longer on your mind.
"She used to walk around the house naked,
Flossing her teeth," someone said of an old lover. At 9 P.M.
A passenger train enters the outskirts of the city
Where the poor live under their low wattage.
A woman in a white bra and half-slip, ironing.
A man in his suit of red long underwear
Slumps over a kitchen table, a glass of
Something near at hand. Commonplace,
Noble because nightly and exposed.

www.ingramcontent.com/pod-product-compliance
Lightning Source LLC
Chambersburg PA
CBHW022346040426
42449CB00006B/736